MUSIC MINUS ONE CLARINET
MUSIC MINUS ONE TRUMPET

CLASSIC THEMES

from Great Composers
-intermediate level-

3245
3837

(2nd-3rd year ability)

Printed in Canad

COMPACT DISC PAGE AND BAND INFORMATION

Music Minus One

Classic Themes
Student Edition Clarinet
Student Edition Trumpet

The Yankee Doodle Boy

Tempo di Marcia

George M. Cohan

3837
3245

Waves Of The Danube

Waltz

1 2/3 piano intro
precedes solo.

Tempo di Valse

J. Ivanovici

D.C. al Fine

3837
3245

Loch Lomond

Andante

Old Scotch Song

Dark Eyes

Gypsy Song

Gold And Silver

Waltz

1 2/3 piano intro
precedes solo.

Franz Lehar

Tempo di Valse

Andantino

Edwin Lemare

3837
3245

Barcarolle
from Tales of Hoffman

2 bar piano intro
precedes solo.

Jacques Offenbach

Allegretto

3837
3245

Beautiful Dreamer

2 bar piano intro
precedes solo.

Stephen Foster

Andantino

mp

3837
3245

Blue Danube

Waltz

Johann Strauss

2 bar piano intro
precedes solo.

Tempo di Valse

3837
3245

Ciribiribin

A. Pestalozza

Come Back To Sorrento

Ernesto Di Curtis

3837
3245

Melody In F

Anton Rubenstein

2 bar piano intro
precedes solo.

Moderato

3837
3245

None But The Lonely Heart

Andante non tanto

Peter I. Tschaikowsky

The Star Spangled Banner

Francis Scott Key

Apache Dance

3 ½ bar piano intro
precedes solo.

Valse moderato

Jacques Offenbach

3837
3245

Tales From The Vienna Woods

Waltz

Tempo di Valse

Johann Strauss

3837
3245

A Media Luz

4 3/8 bar piano intro
precedes solo.

Eduardo Donato

3837
3245

Ave Maria

Andante

Franz Schubert

Country Gardens

4 bar piano solo
precedes solo.

Allegro moderato

English Folk Song

3837
3245

Evening Star

from Tannhausser

Richard Wagner

Andante mosso

3837
3245

Fifth Nocturne

J. Leybach

Humoreske

2 bar piano intro
precedes solo.

Poco lento e grazioso

Anton Dvorak

3837
3245

Slavonic Dance

2 bar piano intro
precedes solo.

Allegretto grazioso

Anton Dvorak

3837
3245

Tango

Andantino grazioso

Isaac Albeniz

3837
3245

Two Guitars

2 bar piano intro
precedes solo.

Andante con moto

Gypsy Melody

3837
3245

Moment Musical

Franz Schubert

Largo
from Xerxes

George F. Handel

3837
3245

MMO Compact Disc Catalog

BROADWAY

____ LES MISERABLES/PHANTOM OF THE OPERA	MMO CD 1016
____ HITS OF ANDREW LLOYD WEBBER	MMO CD 1054
____ GUYS AND DOLLS	MMO CD 1067
____ WEST SIDE STORY 2 CD Set	MMO CD 1100
____ CABARET 2 CD Set	MMO CD 1110
____ BROADWAY HEROES AND HEROINES	MMO CD 1121
____ CAMELOT	MMO CD 1173
____ BEST OF ANDREW LLOYD WEBBER	MMO CD 1130
____ THE SOUND OF BROADWAY	MMO CD 1133
____ BROADWAY MELODIES	MMO CD 1134
____ BARBRA'S BROADWAY	MMO CD 1144
____ JEKYLL & HYDE	MMO CD 1151
____ SHOWBOAT	MMO CD 1160
____ MY FAIR LADY 2 CD Set	MMO CD 1174
____ OKLAHOMA	MMO CD 1175
____ THE SOUND OF MUSIC 2 CD Set	MMO CD 1176
____ SOUTH PACIFIC	MMO CD 1177
____ THE KING AND I	MMO CD 1178
____ FIDDLER ON THE ROOF 2 CD Set	MMO CD 1179
____ CAROUSEL	MMO CD 1180
____ PORGY AND BESS	MMO CD 1181
____ THE MUSIC MAN	MMO CD 1183
____ ANNIE GET YOUR GUN 2 CD Set	MMO CD 1186
____ HELLO DOLLY! 2 CD Set	MMO CD 1187
____ OLIVER 2 CD Set	MMO CD 1189
____ SUNSET BOULEVARD	MMO CD 1193
____ GREASE	MMO CD 1196
____ SMOKEY JOE'S CAFE	MMO CD 1197
____ MISS SAIGON	MMO CD 1226

CLARINET

____ MOZART CONCERTO, IN A, K.622	MMO CD 3201
____ WEBER CONCERTO NO. 1 in Fm. STAMITZ CONC. No. 3 IN Bb	MMO CD 3202
____ SPOHR CONCERTO NO. 1 in C MINOR OP. 26	MMO CD 3203
____ WEBER CONCERTO OP. 26, BEETHOVEN TRIO OP. 11	MMO CD 3204
____ FIRST CHAIR CLARINET SOLOS	MMO CD 3205
____ THE ART OF THE SOLO CLARINET:	MMO CD 3206
____ MOZART QUINTET IN A, K.581	MMO CD 3207
____ BRAHMS SONATAS OP. 120 NO. 1 & 2.	MMO CD 3208
____ WEBER GRAND DUO CONCERTANT WAGNER ADAGIO	MMO CD 3209
____ SCHUMANN FANTASY OP. 73, 3 ROMANCES OP. 94	MMO CD 3210
____ EASY CLARINET SOLOS Volume 1 - STUDENT LEVEL	MMO CD 3211
____ EASY CLARINET SOLOS Volume 2 - STUDENT LEVEL	MMO CD 3212
____ EASY JAZZ DUETS - STUDENT LEVEL	MMO CD 3213
____ VISIONS The Clarinet Artistry of Ron Odrich	MMO CD 3214
____ IN A LEAGUE OF HIS OWN Popular Songs played by Ron Odrich and You	MMO CD 3215
____ SINATRA SET TO MUSIC Kern, Weill, Gershwin, Howard and You	MMO CD 3216
____ STRAVINSKY: L'HISTOIRE DU SOLDAT	MMO CD 3217
____ BEGINNING CONTEST SOLOS - Jerome Bunke, Clinician	MMO CD 3221
____ BEGINNING CONTEST SOLOS - Harold Wright	MMO CD 3222
____ INTERMEDIATE CONTEST SOLOS - Stanley Drucker	MMO CD 3223
____ INTERMEDIATE CONTEST SOLOS - Jerome Bunke, Clinician	MMO CD 3224
____ ADVANCED CONTEST SOLOS - Stanley Drucker	MMO CD 3225
____ ADVANCED CONTEST SOLOS - Harold Wright	MMO CD 3226
____ INTERMEDIATE CONTEST SOLOS - Stanley Drucker	MMO CD 3227
____ ADVANCED CONTEST SOLOS - Stanley Drucker	MMO CD 3228
____ ADVANCED CONTEST SOLOS - Harold Wright	MMO CD 3229
____ BRAHMS Clarinet Quintet in Bm, Op. 115	MMO CD 3230
____ TEACHER'S PARTNER Basic Clarinet Studies	MMO CD 3231
____ JEWELS FOR WOODWIND QUINTET	MMO CD 3232
____ WOODWIND QUINTETS minus CLARINET	MMO CD 3233
____ FROM DIXIE to SWING	MMO CD 3234
____ THE VIRTUOSO CLARINETIST Baermann Method, Op. 63 4 CD Set	MMO CD 3240
____ ART OF THE CLARINET Baermann Method, Op. 64 4 CD Set	MMO CD 3241
____ POPULAR CONCERT FAVORITES WITH ORCHESTRA	MMO CD 3242
____ BAND-AIDS CONCERT BAND FAVORITES WITH ORCHESTRA	MMO CD 3243
____ WORLD FAVORITES Student Editions, 41 Easy Selections (1st-2nd year)	MMO CD 3244
____ CLASSIC THEMES Student Editions, 27 Easy Songs (2nd-3rd year)	MMO CD 3245

PIANO

____ BEETHOVEN CONCERTO NO. 1 IN C	MMO CD 3001
____ BEETHOVEN CONCERTO NO. 2 IN Bb	MMO CD 3002
____ BEETHOVEN CONCERTO NO. 3 IN C MINOR	MMO CD 3003
____ BEETHOVEN CONCERTO NO. 4 IN G	MMO CD 3004
____ BEETHOVEN CONCERTO NO. 5 IN Eb (2 CD SET)	MMO CD 3005

____ GRIEG CONCERTO IN A MINOR OP.16	MMO CD 300■
____ RACHMANINOFF CONCERTO NO. 2 IN C MINOR	MMO CD 300■
____ SCHUMANN CONCERTO IN A MINOR	MMO CD 300■
____ BRAHMS CONCERTO NO. 1 IN D MINOR (2 CD SET)	MMO CD 300■
____ CHOPIN CONCERTO NO. 1 IN E MINOR OP. 11	MMO CD 301■
____ MENDELSSOHN CONCERTO NO. 1 IN G MINOR	MMO CD 301■
____ MOZART CONCERTO NO. 9 IN Eb K.271	MMO CD 301■
____ MOZART CONCERTO NO. 12 IN A K.414	MMO CD 301■
____ MOZART CONCERTO NO. 20 IN D MINOR K.466	MMO CD 301■
____ MOZART CONCERTO NO. 23 IN A K.488	MMO CD 301■
____ MOZART CONCERTO NO. 24 IN C MINOR K.491	MMO CD 301■
____ MOZART CONCERTO NO. 26 IN D K.537, CORONATION	MMO CD 301■
____ MOZART CONCERTO NO. 17 IN G K.453	MMO CD 301■
____ LISZT CONCERTO NO. 1 IN Eb, WEBER OP. 79	MMO CD 301■
____ LISZT CONCERTO NO. 2 IN A, HUNGARIAN FANTASIA	MMO CD 302■
____ J.S. BACH CONCERTO IN F MINOR, J.C. BACH CON. IN Eb	MMO CD 302■
____ J.S. BACH CONCERTO IN D MINOR	MMO CD 302■
____ HAYDN CONCERTO IN D	MMO CD 302■
____ HEART OF THE PIANO CONCERTO	MMO CD 302■
____ THEMES FROM GREAT PIANO CONCERTI	MMO CD 302■
____ TSCHAIKOVSKY CONCERTO NO. 1 IN Bb MINOR	MMO CD 302■
____ ART OF POPULAR PIANO PLAYING, Vol. 1 STUDENT LEVEL	MMO CD 303■
____ ART OF POPULAR PIANO PLAYING, Vol. 2 STUDENT LEVEL 2 CD Set	MMO CD 303■
____ 'POP' PIANO FOR STARTERS STUDENT LEVEL	MMO CD 303■
____ DVORAK TRIO IN A MAJOR, OP. 90 "Dumky Trio"	MMO CD 303■
____ DVORAK QUINTET IN A MAJOR, OP. 81	MMO CD 303■
____ MENDELSSOHN TRIO IN D MAJOR, OP. 49.	MMO CD 303■
____ MENDELSSOHN TRIO IN C MINOR, OP. 66	MMO CD 304■
____ BLUES FUSION FOR PIANO	MMO CD 304■
____ CLAUDE BOLLING SONATA FOR FLUTE AND JAZZ PIANO TRIO	MMO CD 305■
____ TWENTY DIXIELAND CLASSICS	MMO CD 305■
____ TWENTY RHYTHM BACKGROUNDS TO STANDARDS	MMO CD 305■
____ FROM DIXIE to SWING	MMO CD 305■
____ J.S. BACH BRANDENBURG CONCERTO NO. 5 IN D MAJOR	MMO CD 305■
____ BACH Cm CONC. - 2 PIANOS / SCHUMANN & VAR., OP. 46 - 2 PIANOS	MMO CD 305■
____ J.C. BACH Bm CONC./HAYDN C CONCERT./HANDEL CONC. GROSSO-D	MMO CD 305■
____ J.S. BACH TRIPLE CONCERTO IN A MINOR	MMO CD 305■
____ FRANCK SYM. VAR. / MENDELSSOHN: CAPRICCO BRILLANT	MMO CD 30■
____ C.P.E. BACH CONCERTO IN A MINOR	MMO CD 30■
____ STRETCHIN' OUT-'Comping' with a Jazz Rhythm Section	MMO CD 30■
____ RAVEL: PIANO TRIO	MMO CD 30■
____ THE JIM ODRICH EXPERIENCE Pop Piano Played Easy	MMO CD 30■
____ POPULAR PIANO MADE EASY Arranged by Jim Odrich	MMO CD 30■
____ SCHUMANN: Piano Trio in D Minor, Opus 63	MMO CD 30■
____ BEETHOVEN: Trio No. 8 & Trio No. 11, "Kakadu" Variations	MMO CD 30■
____ SCHUBERT: Piano Trio in Bb Major, Opus 99 (2 CD Set)	MMO CD 30■
____ SCHUBERT: Piano Trio in Eb Major, Opus 100 (2 CD Set)	MMO CD 30■
____ POPULAR SONGS Arranged by Jim Odrich	MMO CD 30■

PIANO - FOUR HANDS

____ RACHMANINOFF Six Scenes ... 4-5th year	MMO CD 30■
____ ARENSKY 6 Pieces, STRAVINSKY 3 Easy Dances ... 2-3rd year	MMO CD 30■
____ FAURE: The Dolly Suite	MMO CD 30■
____ DEBUSSY: Four Pieces	MMO CD 30■
____ SCHUMANN Pictures from the East ... 4-5th year	MMO CD 30■
____ BEETHOVEN Three Marches ... 4-5th year	MMO CD 30■
____ MOZART COMPLETE MUSIC FOR PIANO FOUR HANDS 2 CD Set	MMO CD 30■
____ MAYKAPAR First Steps, OP. 29 ... 1-2nd year	MMO CD 30■
____ TSCHAIKOVSKY: 50 Russian Folk Songs	MMO CD 30■
____ BIZET: 12 Children's Games	MMO CD 30■
____ GRETCHANINOFF: ON THE GREEN MEADOW	MMO CD 30■
____ POZZOLI: SMILES OF CHILDHOOD	MMO CD 30■
____ DIABELLI: PLEASURES OF YOUTH	MMO CD 30■
____ SCHUBERT: FANTASIA & GRAND SONATA	MMO CD 30■

VIOLIN

____ BRUCH CONCERTO NO. 1 IN G MINOR OP.26	MMO CD 31■
____ MENDELSSOHN CONCERTO IN E MINOR	MMO CD 31
____ TSCHAIKOVSKY CONCERTO IN D OP. 35	MMO CD 31
____ BACH DOUBLE CONCERTO IN D MINOR	MMO CD 31
____ BACH CONCERTO IN A MINOR, CONCERTO IN E	MMO CD 3
____ BACH BRANDENBURG CONCERTI NOS. 4 & 5	MMO CD 3
____ BACH BRANDENBURG CONCERTO NO. 2, TRIPLE CONCERTO	MMO CD 3
____ BACH CONCERTO IN DM, (FROM CONCERTO FOR HARPSICHORD)	MMO CD 3
____ BRAHMS CONCERTO IN D OP. 77	MMO CD 3
____ CHAUSSON POEME, SCHUBERT RONDO	MMO CD 3
____ LALO SYMPHONIE ESPAGNOLE	MMO CD 3
____ MOZART CONCERTO IN D K.218, VIVALDI CON. AM OP.3 NO.6	MMO CD 3
____ MOZART CONCERTO IN A K.219	MMO CD 3
____ WIENIAWSKI CON. IN D. SARASATE ZIGEUNERWEISEN	MMO CD 3
____ VIOTTI CONCERTO NO. 22 IN A MINOR	MMO CD 3
____ BEETHOVEN 2 ROMANCES, SONATA NO. 5 IN F "SPRING SONATA"	MMO CD 3

MMO Compact Disc Catalog

MMO Compact Disc Catalog

____ THE ART OF THE SOLO TRUMPET with Orchestral Accompaniment ....MMO CD 3807
____ BAROQUE BRASS AND BEYOND Brass Quintets ....MMO CD 3808
____ THE COMPLETE ARBAN DUETS all of the classic studies..........................MMO CD 3809
____ SOUSA MARCHES PLUS BEETHOVEN, BERLIOZ, STRAUSS ....MMO CD 3810
____ BEGINNING CONTEST SOLOS Gerard Schwarz ....MMO CD 3811
____ BEGINNING CONTEST SOLOS Armando Ghitalla ....MMO CD 3812
____ INTERMEDIATE CONTEST SOLOS Robert Nagel, Soloist ....MMO CD 3813
____ INTERMEDIATE CONTEST SOLOS Gerard Schwarz ....MMO CD 3814
____ ADVANCED CONTEST SOLOS Robert Nagel, Soloist ....MMO CD 3815
____ CONTEST SOLOS Armando Ghitalla ....MMO CD 3816
____ INTERMEDIATE CONTEST SOLOS Gerard Schwarz ....MMO CD 3817
____ ADVANCED CONTEST SOLOS Robert Nagel, Soloist ....MMO CD 3818
____ ADVANCED CONTEST SOLOS Armando Ghitalla ....MMO CD 3819
____ BEGINNING CONTEST SOLOS Raymond Crisara ....MMO CD 3820
____ BEGINNING CONTEST SOLOS Raymond Crisara ....MMO CD 3821
____ INTERMEDIATE CONTEST SOLOS Raymond Crisara ....MMO CD 3822
____ TEACHER'S PARTNER Basic Trumpet Studies 1st year ....MMO CD 3823
____ TWENTY DIXIELAND CLASSICS ....MMO CD 3824
____ TWENTY RHYTHM BACKGROUNDS TO STANDARDS ....MMO CD 3825
____ FROM DIXIE TO SWING ....MMO CD 3826
____ TRUMPET PIECES BRASS QUINTETS ....MMO CD 3827
____ MODERN BRASS QUINTETS ....MMO CD 3828
____ WHEN JAZZ WAS YOUNG The Bob Wilber All Stars ....MMO CD 3829
____ CONCERT BAND FAVORITES WITH ORCHESTRA ....MMO CD 3831
____ BAND-AIDS CONCERT BAND FAVORITES WITH ORCHESTRA ....MMO CD 3832
____ BRASS TRAX The Trumpet Artistry Of David O'Neill ....MMO CD 3833
____ TRUMPET TRIUMPHANT The Further Adventures Of David O'Neill ....MMO CD 3834
____ WORLD FAVORITES Student Editions, 41 Easy Selections (1st-2nd year) .....MMO CD 3836
____ CLASSIC THEMES Student Editions, 27 Easy Songs (2nd-3rd year) ....MMO CD 3837
____ STRAVINSKY: L'HISTOIRE DU SOLDAT ....MMO CD 3835
____ 12 CLASSIC JAZZ STANDARDS Bb/Eb/Bass Clef......................................MMO CD 7010
____ 12 MORE CLASSIC JAZZ STANDARDS Bb/Eb/Bass Clef.............................MMO CD 7011

TROMBONE

____ TROMBONE SOLOS Student Level Volume 1 ....MMO CD 3901
____ TROMBONE SOLOS Student Level Volume 2 ....MMO CD 3902
____ EASY JAZZ DUETS Student Level ....MMO CD 3903
____ BAROQUE BRASS & BEYOND Brass Quintets..MMO CD 3904
____ MUSIC FOR BRASS ENSEMBLE Brass Quintets ....MMO CD 3905
____ UNSUNG HERO George Roberts ....MMO CD 3906
____ BIG BAND BALLADS George Roberts ....MMO CD 3907
____ STRAVINSKY: L'HISTOIRE DU SOLDAT ....MMO CD 3908
____ BEGINNING CONTEST SOLOS Per Brevig ....MMO CD 3911
____ BEGINNING CONTEST SOLOS Jay Friedman...MMO CD 3912
____ INTERMEDIATE CONTEST SOLOS Keith Brown, Professor, Indiana U. ......MMO CD 3913
____ INTERMEDIATE CONTEST SOLOS Jay Friedman ....MMO CD 3914
____ ADVANCED CONTEST SOLOS Keith Brown, Professor, Indiana University ..MMO CD 3915
____ ADVANCED CONTEST SOLOS Per Brevig ....MMO CD 3916
____ ADVANCED CONTEST SOLOS Keith Brown, Professor, Indiana University ..MMO CD 3917
____ ADVANCED CONTEST SOLOS Jay Friedman ....MMO CD 3918
____ ADVANCED CONTEST SOLOS Per Brevig ....MMO CD 3919
____ TEACHER'S PARTNER Basic Trombone Studies 1st year ....MMO CD 3920
____ TWENTY DIXIELAND CLASSICS ....MMO CD 3924
____ TWENTY RHYTHM BACKGROUNDS TO STANDARDS ....MMO CD 3925
____ FROM DIXIE TO SWING ....MMO CD 3926
____ STICKS & BONES BRASS QUINTETS ....MMO CD 3927
____ FOR TROMBONES ONLY MORE BRASS QUINTETS ....MMO CD 3928
____ POPULAR CONCERT FAVORITES The Stuttgart Festival Band ....MMO CD 3929
____ BAND-AIDS CONCERT BAND FAVORITES WITH ORCHESTRA ....MMO CD 3930
____ WORLD FAVORITES Student Editions, 41 Easy Selections (1st-2nd year) .....MMO CD 3931
____ CLASSIC THEMES Student Editions, 27 Easy Songs (2nd-3rd year) ....MMO CD 3932
____ 12 CLASSIC JAZZ STANDARDS Bb/Eb/Bass Clef......................................MMO CD 7010
____ 12 MORE CLASSIC JAZZ STANDARDS Bb/Eb/Bass Clef.............................MMO CD 7011

TENOR SAXOPHONE

____ TENOR SAXOPHONE SOLOS Student Edition Volume 1 ....MMO CD 4201
____ TENOR SAXOPHONE SOLOS Student Edition Volume 2 ....MMO CD 4202
____ EASY JAZZ DUETS FOR TENOR SAXOPHONE...MMO CD 4203
____ FOR SAXES ONLY Arranged by Bob Wilber..MMO CD 4204
____ BLUES FUSION FOR SAXOPHONE ....MMO CD 4205
____ JOBIM BRAZILIAN BOSSA NOVAS with STRINGS ....MMO CD 4206
____ TWENTY DIXIE CLASSICS ....MMO CD 4207
____ TWENTY RHYTHM BACKGROUNDS TO STANDARDS ....MMO CD 4208
____ PLAY LEAD IN A SAX SECTION ....MMO CD 4209
____ DAYS OF WINE & ROSES Sax Section Minus You ....MMO CD 4210
____ FRENCH & AMERICAN SAXOPHONE QUARTETS ....MMO CD 4211
____ CONCERT BAND FAVORITES WITH ORCHESTRA ....MMO CD 4212
____ BAND AIDS CONCERT BAND FAVORITES...MMO CD 4213

____ JAZZ JAM FOR TENOR (2 CD Set) ....MMO CD 4214
____ 12 CLASSIC JAZZ STANDARDS Bb/Eb/Bass Clef......................................MMO CD 7010
____ 12 MORE CLASSIC JAZZ STANDARDS Bb/Eb/Bass Clef.............................MMO CD 7011

CELLO

____ DVORAK Concerto in B Minor Op. 104 (2 CD Set) ....MMO CD 3701
____ C.P.E. BACH Concerto in A Minor ....MMO CD 3702
____ BOCCHERINI Concerto in Bb, BRUCH Kol Nidrei ....MMO CD 3703
____ TEN PIECES FOR CELLO ....MMO CD 3704
____ SCHUMANN Concerto in Am & Other Selections ....MMO CD 3705
____ CLAUDE BOLLING Suite For Cello & Jazz Piano Trio ....MMO CD 3706
____ RAVEL: PIANO TRIO MINUS CELLO ....MMO CD 3707
____ RAGTIME STRING QUARTETS ....MMO CD 3708
____ SCHUMANN: Piano Trio in D Minor, Opus 63 ....MMO CD 3709
____ BEETHOVEN: Piano Trio For Cello ....MMO CD 3710
____ SCHUBERT: Piano Trio in Bb Major, Opus 99 Minus Cello (2 CD Set) ....MMO CD 3711
____ SCHUBERT: Piano Trio in Eb Major, Opus 100 Minus Cello (2 CD Set) ....MMO CD 3712
____ BEETHOVEN: STRING QUARTET in A minor, Opus 132 (2 CD Set) ....MMO CD 3713
____ DVORAK QUINTET in A Major, Opus 81 Minus Cello..................................MMO CD 3714

OBOE

____ ALBINONI Concerti in Bb, Op. 7 No. 3, No. 6, D. Op. 9 No. 2 in Dm ....MMO CD 3400
____ TELEMANN Conc. in Fm; HANDEL Conc. in Bb; VIVALDI Conc.in Dm ....MMO CD 3401
____ MOZART Quartet in F K.370, STAMITZ Quartet in F Op. 8 No. 3 ....MMO CD 3402
____ BACH Brandenburg Concerto No. 2, Telemann Con. in Am ....MMO CD 3403
____ CLASSIC SOLOS FOR OBOE Delia Montenegro, Soloist ....MMO CD 3404
____ MASTERPIECES FOR WOODWIND QUINTET ....MMO CD 3405
____ THE JOY OF WOODWIND QUINTETS ....MMO CD 3406
____ PEPUSCH SONATAS IN C/TELEMANN SONATA IN Cm ....MMO CD 3407
____ QUANTZ TRIO SONATA IN Cm/BACH GIGUE/ABEL SONATAS IN F ....MMO CD 3408

ALTO SAXOPHONE

____ ALTO SAXOPHONE SOLOS Student Edition Volume 1 ....MMO CD 4101
____ ALTO SAXOPHONE SOLOS Student Edition Volume 2. ....MMO CD 4102
____ EASY JAZZ DUETS FOR ALTO SAXOPHONE ....MMO CD 4103
____ FOR SAXES ONLY Arranged Bob Wilber ....MMO CD 4104
____ JOBIM BRAZILIAN BOSSA NOVAS with STRINGS ....MMO CD 4105
____ UNSUNG HEROES FOR ALTO SAXOPHONE...MMO CD 4106
____ BEGINNING CONTEST SOLOS Paul Brodie, Canadian Soloist ....MMO CD 4110
____ BEGINNING CONTEST SOLOS Vincent Abato ....MMO CD 4111
____ INTERMEDIATE CONTEST SOLOS Paul Brodie, Canadian Soloist ....MMO CD 4112
____ INTERMEDIATE CONTEST SOLOS Vincent Abato ....MMO CD 4113
____ ADVANCED CONTEST SOLOS Paul Brodie. Canadian Soloist....................MMO CD 4114
____ ADVANCED CONTEST SOLOS Vincent Abato ....MMO CD 4115
____ ADVANCED CONTEST SOLOS Paul Brodie, Canadian Soloist ....MMO CD 4116
____ Basic Studies for Alto Sax TEACHER'S PARTNER 1st year level ....MMO CD 4117
____ ADVANCED CONTEST SOLOS Vincent Abato ....MMO CD 4118
____ PLAY LEAD IN A SAX SECTION ....MMO CD 4120
____ DAYS OF WINE & ROSES/SENSUAL SAX ....MMO CD 4121
____ TWENTY DIXIELAND CLASSICS ....MMO CD 4122
____ TWENTY RHYTHM BACKGROUNDS TO STANDARDS ....MMO CD 4123
____ CONCERT BAND FAVORITES WITH ORCHESTRA ....MMO CD 4124
____ BAND AIDS CONCERT BAND FAVORITES...MMO CD 4125
____ MUSIC FOR SAXOPHONE QUARTET ....MMO CD 4126
____ WORLD FAVORITES Student Editions, 41 Easy Selections (1st-2nd year) .....MMO CD 4127
____ CLASSIC THEMES Student Editions, 27 Easy Songs (2nd-3rd year) ....MMO CD 4128
____ 12 CLASSIC JAZZ STANDARDS Bb/Eb/Bass Clef......................................MMO CD 7010
____ 12 MORE CLASSIC JAZZ STANDARDS Bb/Eb/Bass Clef.............................MMO CD 7011

SOPRANO SAXOPHONE

____ FRENCH & AMERICAN SAXOPHONE QUARTETS ....MMO CD 4801
____ 12 CLASSIC JAZZ STANDARDS Bb/Eb/Bass Clef......................................MMO CD 7010
____ 12 MORE CLASSIC JAZZ STANDARDS Bb/Eb/Bass Clef.............................MMO CD 7011

BARITONE SAXOPHONE

____ MUSIC FOR SAXOPHONE QUARTET ....MMO CD 4901
____ 12 CLASSIC JAZZ STANDARDS Bb/Eb/Bass Clef......................................MMO CD 7010
____ 12 MORE CLASSIC JAZZ STANDARDS Bb/Eb/Bass Clef.............................MMO CD 7011

MMO Music Group • 50 Executive Boulevard, Elmsford, New York 10523, 1-(800) 669-7464
Website: www. minusone.com • E-mail: mmomus@aol.com